GEBO

"where bombs fell
in perfect
iambic pentameter
da DUM da DUM da DUM
da DUM da DUM"

Thom Boulton

Poet Laureate for The City of Plymouth, UK (2016-2020)

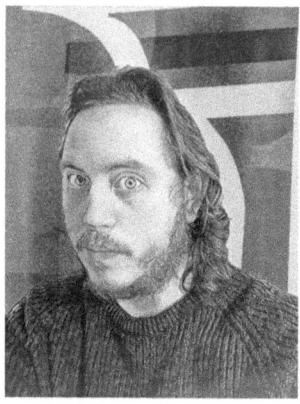

Thom is a regular performer in the South West of England, reading at Cross Country Writers, Wonderzoo, Plymouth Language Club, and The Port Eliot Festival. Over the past few years he has been involved in projects such as the Poppies:Wave artistic response, a robotic poetry collaboration with Volume AI, has sat on the panel for the Mayflower400 cultural bids, and co-produced a weekly poetry slot on Radio Devon during the first UK lockdown.

Other Books:
Prima Materia, (2018)

GEBO

Thom Boulton

GEBO

A SHOALS OF STARLINGS PRESS BOOK

ISBN: 978-1-913767-12-9

Text copyright © Thom Boulton 2021

Cover artwork copyright © Andrew Martin 2021

The rights of Thom Boulton to be identified as the author of this work has been asserted by Shoals of Starlings Press

All rights are reserved. No part of this book may be used or reproduced in any matter whatsoever without written permission from the author, except in the case of brief quotations embodied in critical articles or reviews.

First published in 2021

Shoals of Starlings Press logo is copyright © Andrew Martin 2020

Shoals of Starlings Press is based in Plymouth, UK

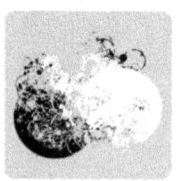

Shoals
of
Starlings
Press

CONTENTS

Apocalypse	9
The Gift	17
Occultists and Poets	18
Entropy Demands to Know Your Phone Number	20
Butterfly	23
Do You Look at the Moon When I Look at the Moon?	24
On a Dead Man Buried at the Crossroads	26
Monkey Paw	28
I Am Why Your Ghost No Longer Speaks	29
Living in the Unwritten Scores	31
Silver Bullet	32
Running out of Gravity	33
The Missing Chapters	35
Paper Plane	36
I Saw Your Wish Today	37
Thread	39
Carry Us Home	41
This Poem Will Never Be Read	43
Lost in the Colourless Graves of its Reflection	46
We Ate the Stars and Spat Out Their Dust	49
Resurrection	51

Apocalypse

Drawn curtains
fasten their threads together
never to open again

the pattern does not complete
if not aligned

each chink or fold leaning into the other

Sun's eyes flutter
to brighten the roads
  better than a lick of paint
  better than licking a battery
these jolts will restart the traffic
if only they can navigate
the pot holes and speed bumps
via alternate routes

This must be what summer feels like

And great star, named and unnamed
capturing gaze
yet the cornea do not burn
like they told every froglet
instilled in the pond

distilled in the factories

live it – eat it – pray it – believe it
(you better not believe it)

this scorching sun
sitting in the sky's thoughts
staring down, near enough
to give life to a clump of rock

this sun, inventing time
by parking its arse-cheeks
on the ground
split pantyhose
generate a shadow
around revealed flesh

Seasons of comfort are in session

Goldilocks declares
on the street corners of
The Republic of Poetry – how
it is just right

The shy trees are no more – they
yell jokes from a cannibalistic book
made of their skin
each punchline lands an honest mark

on the face

Somewhere, a statue of a lion whimpers
with its thorn-laced paw
soothed by the tender talons
of a bird of prey – pluck the stick
fuck the splinters
pluck the crone from the maiden's head
as winds
tighten, and tease your throat

Twin bridges
slumped on the River Tamar
filled with silent excuses
to bolt their cables
into a patch of concrete
suspend disbelief
that the inanimate can pass for being human
tread with caution
for a high volume of gendered vehicles
pass this way

hands from the river
claw onto the bank
with Mother Tenacity's affirming grip

the body of Babylon
scooped up in a length of ribbon

dried in a bath towel
kissed on the forehead and sung to sleep

'my bonny lies over a notion…'

where fresh bed sheets
touch static against spines
a taste of seasonal freedom
cruel as the taste of Midsummer Day's goodnight

sleep tight, for now until the turning

Distant suns
replace the glow of proximity
blinking messages through the blackness
into Morpheus's shorthand
typed into dark wanderings
which countdown
to a wake that breaks the mourning

seductive dreams coloured in crayon
until heat melts the wax
sends a hard vibration
through mortal pages
punctuated by prophecy - the end of all days

sat apart
blurry are the smiles

this is the mask

that hides the face

of the spectre of things to be sung

O GREAT REVELATION!

John the Apostle

John the Beatle

Yer Blues blasts loud into the ear

a meeting is scheduled

in the living rooms

of each depredated domicile

dissemination

will dictate the insemination of The Saviour

or the dragon that fell from a city in the clouds

and then silence

And then more silence

The voiceless assemble
in under an hour – rapid response
this is it folks
the moment

THE END OF ALL DAYS HAS COME!

Bled realities flatline – leylines narrow
every channel dried-up and void

The freaks shall inherit The Sun

Demand it ends its exercise routine
 no-more will it rise to offer high-fives
 to drifting angelic forms
 no-more will it be eaten by the groves
 in their grooves as they spin

The Sun pricks its finger
and sleeps one thousand years
cries a thousand more tears
which
evaporate every millisecond
on the burning surface of corruption

Floods eventually consume soils
a sphere sits on the shoulder of a giant

as it trudges through
fresh formed swamps

the pebble stones of the pavement
beat
with a time-signature of 4/4
with lots of ghost notes scattered

Hovering on the edge of their seats
the gods look down
chortle and choke

it is hard to swallow

what remains is a wasteland

And the only hope of ascension
lies in the footnotes of an unwritten poem

a poem worth dying for.

The Gift

The gods sent you wrapped in
pomegranate leaves
I wrote your location on the back of a breeze
but I lost it

(nothing happens)

in the graves, once sore remnants
hold their breath
it rains, collects on my brow
and floods the vision

cut this polythene bag in my head
drain the water down the sink hole
frantically sorting waste from recycling
get the house in order before the guests arrive

every dip into the purple, silk bag
pulls out a thorn

you'll remove it if it hasn't dislodged
a promise written.

Occultists and Poets

The OCCULTISTS and POETS gather
summoning meaty traumas
to lay on the ground like tinted snowflakes

each memory converses with the one before it
collated into a notebook
and left on the shelf of a library by the sea

the water expands into the senses
as midnight sneaks upon the clock

upon the ground, OCCULTISTS and POETS
birth a sigil of a dragonfly
surrounded by the godly cadavers of innocence

rotting entices a blanket of transcendental fungus to mature

chew on the mushrooms
each crunch a bit of a divine fractal –
this is the time of love and living
how the tree throbs
and the ground wettens with anticipation

the dragonfly animates and manifests
a multiverse of ordinary and extraordinary
where the nephilim are sired

from the daughters of man, wholeheartedly besotted
with the Sons of Heaven

At the cooler end of the day
OCCULTISTS and POETS blend a novel necromancy
resurrecting Edgar Allen Poe's stiff neck
so he can finally finish writing his Twilight fan-fiction

they challenge Poe, speaking out
"You! You're over 18. It's illegal to still be an emo."

An omelette is offered during the ritual
served on a two-dimensional plate
straight from the mind of Mrs Humpty Dumpty

does she cluck or does she suck?
Humpty Dumpty doesn't have a fucking clue
too busy going solo with molly
hitting the electric boogie train at the 24hour disco dive

the notorious resting ground
for all OCCULTISTS and POETS.

Entropy Demands to Know Your Phone Number

Whereby the fundamental pillars of the grand construct
are the golden feathers of a downed plane, the seal
as it violates the penguin, Harry Truman as a shoe-in
for the Right-Honourable Reverend Mayhem, great
Apollo's gait - his flaming genitals that guide the ships
and the fifth quintessence makes itself known

know me, thy name is rebellion

the emerging atom, apple of my "Oh my!"
The physical avatar of ancient fires lit by the kiss of titans
locked in a box and guarded by nine sisters
of an abbey built on snake skins
shredded fore-skins planted to grow new fruits

Oh, rotted corpse, you crawl towards the splintered ray
striking through the canopies of confusion, grown by these
wide-eyed gardeners, securing their hedgerows
their bountiful crops

the problems of the many gods
outweigh
the problems of the one-god

Tell me, where have all the cowboys gone?
John Wayne emits light as he sleeps in the ground

energetic enough to transform black and white, to colour
how predictable, how prestigious, how

how many laws conserve and how many increase?
This rate of unsustainable growth is super unsustainable
entropy demands to know your phone number, says to
stay in touch despite the angle of your face

a whole new world waits in a songbook
readers are sucked in and absorbed, their given names
given a resting place on memorials
veterans of the anomaly
get out your message before it is too late, carry it
sweetly, swaddled, and give it lullabies to drink
undetected
couldn't possibly
couldn't possibly be

the distinctive mass of a raised fist
will not be shipped on the planes
will not grip the cock
will not fist bump in the shadow of a red buttoned cardigan
will not punch the sea to sink the whale

this tiny life
an illusion caused by a blip on the screen
flashing in and out of chapters of Descartes
unattainable

your ghostly pull
posing duplicity
your coy lady craving

in the rising of the moon
the skies connect to the cosmic comforter

opening to stare
opening to welcome

time changes for it is time and the measure of change

rigidity, be the raven of rebellion
and dampen history's birth right.

Butterfly

the flutter of a brown argus
invokes rapid palpitations

drawn to such beauty
that fingers extend to touch

it rests on the tip of wanting
spread wings to drink sunlight

a breeze pauses to draw breath
dew descends down the stem

this moment cannot be kept
but leaves an impression in the soul

Do You Look at the Moon When I Look at the Moon?

A slave to the incandescent eye of fate
cast over my body
examining each line to draw conclusions
that the grandeur of a gilded heart
can be dwarfed by existential silence

penetrates every droplet of the soaked clouds
star-walking choirs pool and chorus
their hymn books written in Hebrew
when none of them read Hebrew

Every page stuck to the one before it
turning a corner in the story
forces the slab of words
to crush and press weak fingers

error is, error is marginal
intent unknown
a country waiting to be discovered
when nobody wants it discovered

Remain distant, let your mewling echo
into a stiff chamber of rib bones
wrapping around a diamond
rought, cut from the flesh of a grounded angel

fallen from the side of the divine, fallen

Do you look at The Moon when I look at The Moon?

On a Dead Man Buried at the Crossroads

There is a revolution but the angry teeth
don't know what they're biting

firefighters cleaning fires

I am the chemicals

The average combustible
engulfs
sticks of lard and beers

spontaneous is the early morning fox
his diet consists
of the rough kiss of the winds
an icy stare to fuck souls
and an assortment of angst riddled migraines

scalped by a lathe
knot, cut against the grain

extramundane taxidermists betting
on if it will stand
or if more glue should be applied to the feet

Great spirits scream into the leaves

shaking the sturdiest of organic structures

hear the voices, they are making demands
on a dead man buried at the crossroads

no deal. Deal
  no deal

make up your fucking minds
make up your backstory
make up - the moment I wake up - made up
of letters and numbers - trickster. Compound

 Taste the air - this freshness declared
claimed by the goddess of longevity
to feed as supper to the sleeping sun.

Monkey Paw

how your fingers curled as you made that wish
coiled melody escaped the tongue
interlocked eyes and two dreamers
casting spells to ensure longevity

the sun will not settle, burns more with each spin
tracing hands on the seams of shadows
praying to the gods of a forgotten time

as the blissful tune goes dormant
the percussion endures
each thump a crack of thunder to wake giants

sleepers stir and gather to lift the skies
hold the heavens to pause the rains
let the soil breathe, the storms pass

and the seas settle into a new universe
held by a tenacious claw.

I Am Why Your Ghost No Longer Speaks

Your ghost walks by my side
chills iron bars to keep me waking

we navigate the paving slab's follicles
where trees protrude
and clutter The Gray Man's face with green

wise to the woes of Orpheus
the pallid words of his poem

we do not turn; will not turn

cut a finger off to make a compass
whittle down the failed flesh
let it spin, let it spin

This is the street where bombs fell
in perfect iambic pentameter
da DUM da DUM da DUM da DUM da DUM

I am coarse like shrapnel
lodged in the sod

I am why the trees wish to escape
abnormal invading presence

I am why your ghost no longer speaks

staves of an unfinished song tied in knots
syncopated rhythms and a cosmic reunion

Take comfort in faith
as a companion
not in an unmade godhead
but in the all-seeing eye
holy ward - I am waiting

until swallowed by the sallow tears
of the heavens
hand in hand with a deadened dream.

Living in the Unwritten Scores

Scarlet voice, the line is dead
a love off the hook and placed on its side

monotonous tones cascade
reject star signs, travels halted

each visit to a reserved space
reveals a woodland where every tree touches

here, no trickster can play games
and a want is enacted, lived bliss

Come the skies waking yawns
eyes close, brace the harsh dapple of day

living in the unwritten scores
that serenade actuality, slumber in euphoria.

Silver Bullet

When constructing reality
my father would produce
a silver tape measure
carefully place its metal tooth
on the glue-board, pull back, then
fire the silver bullet
across the expanse of our front room

Time is a weighty rock
thrown through the window of space
something to marvel
tracking the decay of a fledgling's feathers
a severed apple still breathing
flames choking atop the cake
counting the meridian line as it hums.

Running out of Gravity

Infantilised construct
the maker, the shaper

how the dislodged crawl on the Earth
she to gather into a bundle, sold at market
to the old man with the fat fob watch
pronouncing them all dead at the scene

the eye of Horus
watching, the hand of Thoth, scribes

momentarism, you manifest
our gods of the Nile to run through us
run
run your mouth
run, da-doo run-run

we are running out of gravity
this is why the children's book is upside-down

we are running to what scares us
and labelling quiet evenings curled up
as the stuff that nightmares are made of

we run to the moon but cannot breathe

the rocket moves towards the Earth
they will either drop, burn-up, Happy New
Year, or continue

                        accelerate forward through the very core

                                          popping the crusts
                                        sliding out the wound
                                    to reach the other side.

The Missing Chapters

as if the preface were written on her lips
a deathless tale enacted by two celestials

the taste of rich air as words escape
and two shadows comfortably overlap

reflections in the window cast premonitions
unnamed readers antagonise the ending

the missing chapters caught by the air
and left restless in the hedgerows

words fade in the light of the passing days
the ones that cling to the paper utter prayers

if only hope were an embodied goddess
not simply a blanch on mortal dreams

Paper Plane

Riding through a rainbow
on a paper plane

how I would love to take you
from our spot, looking on

at the restless and measured
devout in the embrace

as we soar further to the edge.

I Saw Your Wish Today

The watcher of time
a supermoon falling into the sting of a tale
baffled by the foot of reality

cascading delight - a cathedral of rays - stained glass
plummeting through the roof, to a graveyard of flowers

lay in the blurred pastels, sink - sink -
a smudge covered blanket swallowing

deeper into the chasm of deification
where an engraved stone slab screams into your soul

open me - open this
an ounce of grounded pollen from the Mother's pestle and mortar

this is idleness - a fire in the arms, Midas smelts
but this form melts all that pass through its hold

in the never-ending pit, a headline written across every wall
any news is news

the half starved would trade words for sustenance
would snap their thoughts for a moment of contiguity

where a heavy idea rests on the chest

listening to the heartbeat of a new being, striking into existence

The watcher sees time tied securely at both ends
tied to the goddess of creativity
but this sallow refutes sorrow
casts its arms up to the empyrean realm

HEAVENLY SPECTRES! GREAT STAR-SERPENT!
Release the strangle, let lungs fill with a new covenant
and not indignation

that no matter the burden of carrying a smile on the spine
 this life, this one

is where petals do not fall but reach for immortality
    where the connection from navel to navel symbolises strength
    where happiness is a borderless country in place of a flag

release time so its watcher may resume journaling
 every perfect and imperfect detail

until time brings him in close
and carries his name into the book of no-shadows.

Thread

Cut out this ravelled thread

so tender eyes numb
to night's cursed brilliance

so visions of torment
may be caught in its web

meet me in the split seconds

where anxious questions
steal away and bide their time

where lifetimes can be lived
in the privacy of delusion

let each pathway lead along the coastline
now our feet may bump into each other

take us to the safety of a strain
composed by engorged fervour

let the deity who was there at our genesis
watch on as two birds fly to the expanse
trembling wings conjuring a new star
as they manifest their own small world

to take its position

and revolve

around a beacon of near-immortal heat

there are no sounds

no locks

just a forever

commanding the seasons

consuming the winds and waves

until all that is left

is a tangled spark

of predilection and wholeness.

Carry Us Home

Were we dead
on lamenting shores
where spent bodies
gaze at the moon
and burn in its reflection
caught by the rocks
bones broken
washed up dolls
caked in wet sand
then there beyond
near the knolls
of dried grasses
a sparrow hawk waits
to carry us home.

Let's fake our deaths
eyes that do not blink
make a holy dream
never dissevered
hearts heavy as quartz
finally resting
on a hot bed of earth.

Our dusk-blue kisses
roars wild as the moon

taken and folded

staved hungers

flesh sewn together

touching the depths

of a craving

an ecstasy

a craving

to carry us home.

This Poem Will Never Be Read

You shaped pain into a boiled sweet
lodged it in the throat, waited for it
to choke and choke and oh god, oh he's
dead - dead - he's dead - he's dead as the
faded colour
of a sun bleached memory, hung
on the wall to shame, pride of place so
that obstinate voices posing as dinner guests
may prod and poke at the tint - look at the tint
oh, this tint is off-ish, this tint is awful

of all you could have done, of every
inch along the naked form of possibility, you chose
the empty graves of a forgotten fate, confessor
death and deity, your tomb as a church -
pray daily and forgive us our sins as we
intoxicate ourselves on the wines of never-cared

all the saints -
where are your gods of poetry now?
They, eating their paper thin rice cakes - no
substance, no substance abuse
skip a heartbeat and offer it up as a token
wish you were here- wish you were there
you are not there –

writer, this poem will never be read
tease out the kilogram weights
from the legs of a lame horse
dragged about the city streets by its face

messiah, this poem will never be read
it is the notes lifted
from an abandoned symphony
offering a reason to the religious treason against
the gifts of the gods of poetry

ritual - cruel ritual

take away these arteries and
foster each drop of blood to a good home

dethroned messenger, remind us the world is fat
and fucked and has gone on too long

we the famine
we the warring, spectacular mercenaries

broke the piggy bank and sold the broken crockery to
the devil

your cruel ritual
so cruel

how the black chip flips to white
how it can be reversed

only the lonely understand maths

make the day sacred
then rewrite the definition of day, and sacred

kissing the face
knowing honey is thicker than water
but neither merit
their own internal systems

this is dryness
this is lastingness

no more will you haunt
the thick tomes of night's splendour

no more will you infect
the breathing lungs to make weak

this is where the sea parts
like a double crown
and drowns your face

this is the end.
 Now. Here.

Lost in the Colourless Graves of its Reflection

The broken morning does not want to wake
it is tired of dreaming
a vision of one hand reaching for the clouds
to pull them free of their endless drift

it is tired of conjuring
a box filled with fresh fruit to graze upon
gaze upon this sufferance - affection of a grape
from the vines of veins that carry love
pumping through flesh and tissues and organs
infected in every inch like the rot forced by time

the broken morning shatters its soul
with every truth
with every day
lost to the devout record keepers and their texts
it aches, is aching
wishing for a muscle relaxant, bind the ribs
crush each nerve in its face

sleep is a prisoner
subjected to reoccurring punishment over
nourishment
this is the hunger strike that strikes the clock
to remind it is now one hour later

the presence of beauty forces mortality
to hold its feet in waters of wanting

the shimmers on the surface
letting out realities in pockets
to fold and follow
a current leading to a sea, to an ocean

The broken morning is tortured
by these frozen waters
desperate to numb each blink
slow the pains of sentience
aware it is gripped

let the morning drown in the sea
lost in the colourless graves of its reflection

hope is for fools; a fools game

it cries out "Carry me! Carry me back to the eclipse."
Months before the birth of a maiden made from flowers

it begs "Bind my eyes to that darkness."

Then the touch of a favourite song will not be quantified
by the knowing look of two apparitions
in search of corporeal form

there can be no more autumns, falling leaves will
never kiss the ground, never drink the horizon
nor share the same air as a revenant

remain a revenant
live out each cycle of the Earth, split in silence
the absence
unaware a muse shifts its shape to fly
into belief
resting in the centre of a morning
already broken by the bird's call.

We Ate the Stars and Spat Out Their Dust

No mourners gather
nobody knows where the body is buried

somewhere between the never-ending woods
and the rivers of aeon
sits a rutting stag
its bawling will sink harts
feint tremors as the crowns clash

war comes through song
not the empty shells or maimed mannequins you spy
but the fight, the passion
climb the stars and slice the head of Chaos from its coiled body

We ate the stars and spat out their dust
we claimed its name and rode the waves

The shaman's drum, sharpened by the night
piercing the fabric of your reality
hear its calling echo throughout eternity
   a pulse to knock a comet out the heavens and into the waters
   a rhythm to stir and drag the rocks from the river bed

warrior – half wake; half dead
boots caked in a gentle layer of mud
used to shape a mortal frame, keep it contained

and yet it yearns
and yet it burns brightly
wanting to escape the restless parade of
chained wrists and tangled tongues

ripped from a hybrid's womb
painted on the side of a bowl
take your labours and trade them for wishes

the djinn have fled the nest, returned to pandemonium

rub your heal with cream to prevent cracks
keep your earphones buried to dull the sullen sirens

and as your back breaks
and the sky falls
and the seas rise
and the land loses itself in both

then you can rest, knowing
your unrealised shape
has two fingers pinching its head.

Resurrection

Out of kennings
chaos magick dictates to cut your lyrics
rearrange them to fit your ears

where are the deadly gallows?
To cure a man of death, hang him there and let him die again
slice his thigh with a spear made of frosted metal
cold touch – cold touch

9 days quickly becomes 9 months
gestation scuppers the bread of your supper
in a stew made for ceremonial purposes

you can't know the runes, their gift, without sacrifice

what's in a union made of cravings?
Salt lines the wound
heart attacks are more likely
when it stops, it will lacerate, form patterns like a spiral

Dominion
There is only one dragon in the bible and his name is Dragon

If pain dictates temperance then we're all fucked
diligence is required
but cannot actualise

when the hoofs of a seven legged horse
stamp across each vertebrae
lined up and waiting for the higher self to open

out of coin
slice your bone into segments
burn your sadness upon each one
start a currency that isn't accepted anywhere

bankers leaving the temple
priests leaving the brothels

the world is back-to-front and inside-out
and if you can't picture it
then imagine your pockets are pulled out
and stuffed behind a radiator
to ensure they're dry by tomorrow

and tomorrow
when will you resurrect?

The necromancers are all unemployed and desperate for work
scoop a handful
sprinkle them on your pudding or Pad Thai

kick your teeth into the bite
let your taste buds sample your hopes

it's been said but perhaps you weren't paying attention
you cannot resurrect the dead without them first dying

Death defier
ignore conventions
know you have no control over the rains
or where they fall

this is your moment to ask
your moment passed, how do you feel?

Someone feed the man
he's been dead so long
he's forgotten how to breathe
and if you remind him
he'll want to do it again

Your raven sylph
   taking a hand to guide to the otherworld
   taking the head with your scythe

could you not have waited?

The saints and sinners have gathered their bacon
cooked it on the back of the Sun
the smell will infiltrate your memories and cling

resurrected

you are resurrected

now what?

Return to the field, pole through your arms
scare away flocks of death as they glide past the rows of crops
or return to the beginning
or return to the middle
or keep waiting for the end. The end. The end again

Waiting. Always waiting. You are always waiting

Your plated shins weigh you down
not enough room on the beach for both voyagers

one will gaze; the other will enter a retrograde phase

neither will live
not until

and even then
not unless.

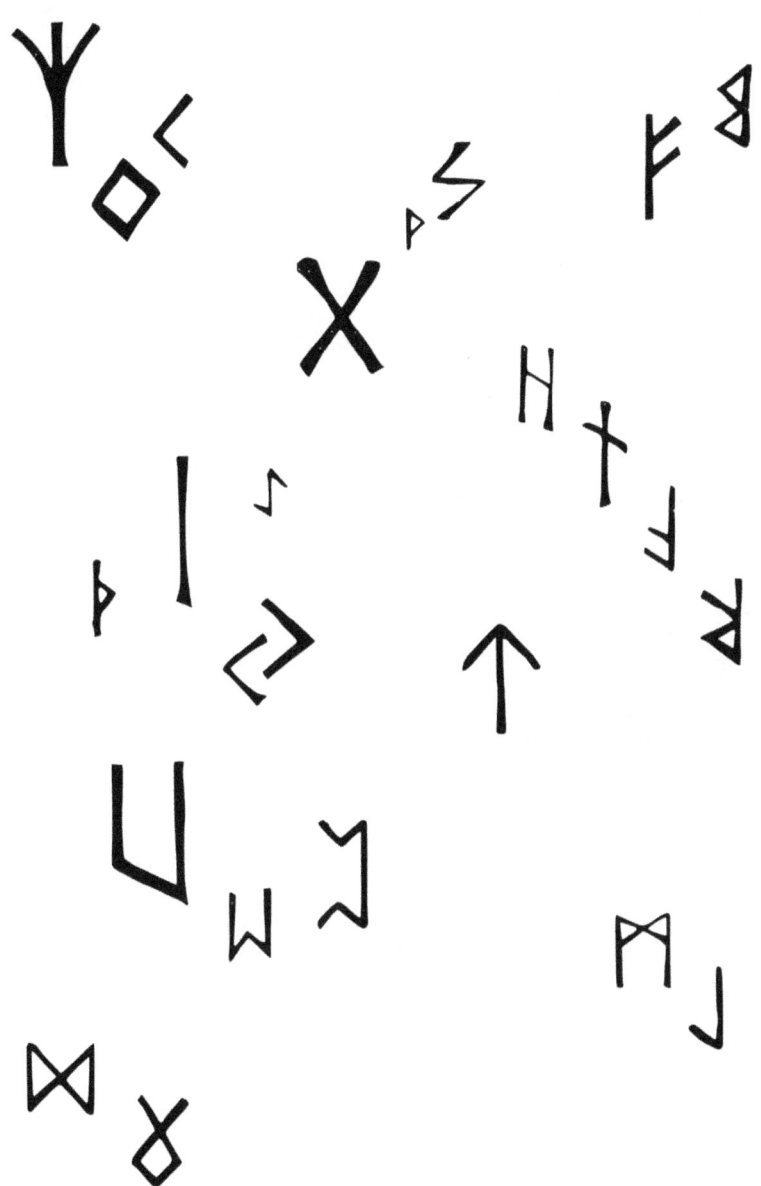

the REST of this PAGE is INTENTIONALLY left BLANK

www.ingramcontent.com/pod-product-compliance
Lightning Source LLC
Chambersburg PA
CBHW022125040426
42450CB00006B/847